ST CUTHBERT'S WAY

Stephen Platt

www.leveretpublishing.com

St Cuthbert's Way
First published - July 2025
Published by Leveret Publishing
56 Covent Garden, Cambridge, CB1 2HR, UK

St Cuthbert's Cross

ISBN 978-1-912460-75-5

© Stephen Platt 2025

All rights reserved. No part of this publication may be reproduced, stored in a retrieval system or transmitted in any form by any means, electronic, mechanical, photocopying, recording or otherwise, except brief extracts for the purpose of review, without the written permission of the publisher.

ST CUTHBERT'S WAY 2025

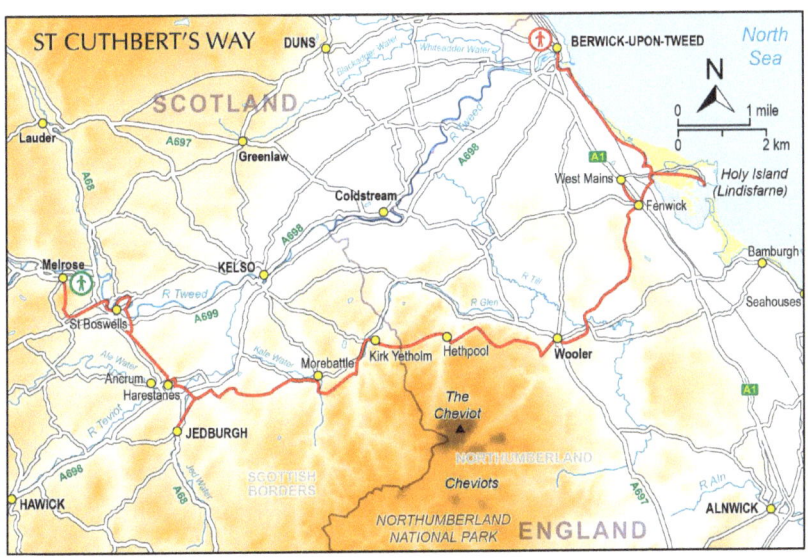

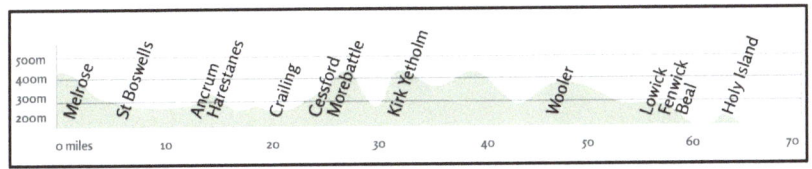

Day 1 Melrose to St Boswell's

Sunday, 11 May

At the station in Sheffield, I had time for a coffee and croissant, and to read the Sunday papers. The train was full, but the journey passed easily, and soon I was crossing the Tweed into Berwick on the Royal Border railway bridge. A compact, dependable place with its pink ashlar sandstone walls and red-tiled roofs, befitting its role as a fortified border town. More Scottish than English, perhaps not surprising, given it changed hands more than a dozen times in the 200 years between 1300 and 1500.

The bus stop was right outside the station and 10 minutes before it was due to leave, a bus stopped nearby. I assumed the driver was having his break and would stop and pick us up, but he sailed past. I waved, and he stopped and I asked him if he was going to Melrose. He was so I and the

Berwick Old Bridge and Quayside

other passengers who had been waiting got on. We recrossed the river over the New Bridge and could look over the Old Berwick stone bridge to the quayside walls and the mighty Tudor ramparts on down the estuary to the sea. The sky and the river were the same clear blue and it felt good to be setting off on another little adventure. I dozed on the bus, despite the potholes and the bumpy ride between Kelso and St Boswells and we rattled and shook along the A699 into St Boswells, a pretty red sandstone village.

In Melrose, I walked around the abbey before setting off up the hill. Melrose Abbey, founded by Cistercian monks in 1136, is a partial ruin, but the stone tracery of the east and south gables and windows is particularly fine. The heart of Robert the Bruce, brought back from crusade in the Holy Land, is thought to be buried here. Located on one of the main roads from Edinburgh south, made Melrose vulnerable to raiding English armies, and the abbey was destroyed by Edward II in 1322, by Richard II in 1385 and by Henry VIII in 1544. This is not, however, the abbey founded by Saint Aidan of Lindisfarne, where Saint Cuthbert trained as a young novice and became prior. That is Old Mailros, situated two miles east, on a

Melrose Abbey

bend in the River Tweed.

The way climbs south over the Eildon Hills. Two thousand years ago the Votadini tribe had their fort or 'oppidum' on the summit of North Eildon. I left the main road and headed up a long flight of steep wooden steps that got me panting and I stopped at a strangely ugly carved bench. The hillside is golden with billowy yellow gorse, scenting strongly of coconut. The land is dry, and the muddy path is baked hard and dry. The views north towards Edinburgh open up. It's not that far to the col between North and Middle Eildon where I stop and take off my sack and lie on the grass for a few minutes before dropping down through beech woods. On past a field of squabbling rooks, to the delightful village of Bowden. The path is trim and well-maintained, with Cuthbert's Cross signs marking the way, the gates held fast with forged Northumberland gate-hooks. Simple and effective. Bowden village is well-kept, with the grass mown, and the houses are spick and span. Sandstone masonry, some ashlar, some rough, but all tightly bonded in a variety of styles. There is an ancient hexagonal water pump, alas, dry, since I could just do with a cool drink. The path leads from the village and drops down a leafy lane to a stream. Over a

Flight of wooden steps leaving Melrose

footbridge across Bowden Burn that reflects the bright green foliage. Birdsong of thrush and robin, scent of May blossom and petals strewn along the path like confetti. A wooden bridge across a stream with young trout in the clear water. The final stretch is along a road into Newton and the Dryberg Arms, where I'll spend the night.

The innkeeper, Leanne, is a cheery young woman with bright red lips and a big smile. She was most welcoming. I had a shower and rang the Thai restaurant she'd recommended for a takeaway, but there was no answer. So I found a Chinese restaurant that would deliver Peking duck and special rice, much too much food, and ate in the lounge.

Octagonal water pump, Bowden

Gorse on ascent to Eildon Hills

Eildon Hill North

Beech woods below Eildon

Bowden Burn

Eildon Hills

River Tweed

Day 2 Newton to Jedburgh

Monday 12 May

The Dryberg Arms is an old-fashioned pub with a pool table and a darts board. Leanne runs it singlehandedly and is ready to serve breakfast. I can't resist always ordering more than I can eat – two poached eggs, black pudding, tomatoes and a potato cake. I set off soon after nine. The path from Newtown to St Boswells goes through woods filled with birdsong. I can hear a chattering wren, a song thrush and robin, a tree creeper and a garden warbler. Beech mast and nut casings scatter the path and there is a distant knocking of a woodpecker in the far distance. There are silver glimpses of the broad river through the trees, but alas, no view of the ruins of Dryburgh Abbey on the opposite bank. There is a suspension Bridge at Dryburgh, and I could have crossed the river here to visit the abbey if I'd read the guidebook. The path climbs wooden stairways to

Dryberg Abbey ruin, 1150

Site of old Melrose Abbey

Suspension Bridge at Dryberg

Typical masonry, St Boswells

The Old Manse, Braehead Road, St Boswells

traverse sections where the trees come down to the water. I'm finding it tiring climbing the steps despite my pack being the lightest it's ever been on a long walk. The margin bordering the path is alive with flowers – red campion, wild garlic, the pretty white stars of stitchwort.

The book shop I've heard about in St Boswells is closed, unfortunately. Before heading down to the River Tweed, which meanders around the village, I stop briefly at a bench against the wall of a large house with the circular corner turret that is popular here in the Borders. Swallows circle above me and perch on the electricity line. The golf course by the river is beautifully mown, and small parties of men with golfing trolleys are strung out along it. Wire fences hem the path through the water meadow, but it doesn't matter; it's such a lovely day, perfect for walking. Fishermen are casting for salmon. At Mertoun Mill weir, a heron stands patiently still. I expect it to fly off when I point my stick, but it's indifferent. The River Tweed is wide here, but shallow because of the drought. The path follows a sweeping bend in the river and gets back nearly to where I started.

Maxton Parish Church is dedicated to St Cuthbert. There has been a church on this site for over 1000 years. It was closed and marketed for

Angler in River Tweed fishing for salmon

Mertoun Bridge

Crystal Well below Benrig House

Maxton Parish Church

Beech hedge from Maxton

sale by the Church of Scotland in January 2025.

From Maxton village, there is a tedious stretch of road bordered by the most amazing beech hedge. It must be ancient. It's a mile long and beautifully trimmed. Deer Street, the Roman road from York to Edinburgh, is waymarked by the sign of a Roman soldier's helmet. It runs parallel to the A68, is, mercifully, a meandering grassy path, sufficiently distant from the main road for the traffic noise to be less intrusive. St Cuthbert would have used Dere Street as it was one of the few well-made roads in the area. I stop for lunch on a grassy verge in the sun, before climbing to a ridge, the site of the battle of Ancrum in 1545. An English army of 5,000 sent by Henry VIII, on its way to Jedburgh after plundering Melrose Abbey, was routed by a Scots army of less than half the size. Standing on Lilliard's Edge I tried to imagine the action. I'd read that the English were on higher ground and attacked south west into the setting sun. Feigning retreat, the Scots had lured the English cavalry to advance ahead of the infantry. The main Scottish army attacked in force as the horses reached the marshy ground due south of the ridge. 700 Borderers in the English army changed sides and the English were routed. These Borderers, including Ker Clan

River Fangu Tuarelli

men from nearby Cessford, were mercenaries or 'free-lancers' owing allegiance to those, either Scottish or English, who would pay them and who were likely to win. Lady Lilliard's stone marks the site, a coffin-shaped monument at the end of the ridge nearest to Dere Street.

I'm tired now and my toes ache with arthritis, but I press on for 4-5 kilometres along the dead straight Dere Street. The path enters a pine wood and there is a strong resinous and citrus scent of pine. There is less birdsong and little understory. Dozens of trees have been felled in the recent storm Arwen in November 2021. Northumberland was particularly badly hit because, unusually, the wind came from the north-east. A party of Canadians is having a tea break on logs by the side of the path. Again, having failed to consult a guidebook in advance, I missed deviating from the route a few hundred metres to visit the Harestanes Centre. Nor do I climb Peniel Heugh to pay my respects to the Waterloo Monument, the pillar I've been viewing from afar. The pillar, in the form of an obelisk, collapsed a year after its construction and a second pillar in the 'manly form' of a Doric column was erected in its stead.

The path drops down to the river Teviot, and I find a route map of St

Dere Street, Roman Road from York to Edinburgh and possibly beyond

Waterloo Monument on Peniel Heugh 237m

Dere Street near Harriets Field

Cuthbert's Way that someone must have dropped. The river is crossed by a long suspension bridge built in 1999 after the previous bridge was damaged in floods. I stop on the other side, take off my boots and socks, and paddle. It's not far now, and the path by the river through the meadows is wonderfully easy. Finally, I meet the road where I plan to leave St Cuthbert's Way and walk into Jedburgh for the night. I'm tired and don't fancy the 3-mile walk into town, so I try hitching. A man comes over. I recognise him as belonging to the party of Canadians I'd met in the woods. He tells me that they are a church party from Toronto that's on a pilgrimage, and he offers me a lift in their coach, which they are waiting for. Some of the group look tired, and they are using the coach to ferry those who can't complete each stage. I ask if anyone has lost a map, and a woman who is guiding a blind woman pipes up that it's hers. She's most grateful. The coach takes us to the door of the Royal Hotel, where I'm staying. The receptionist, a rather stuffy man, asked me to take off my boots before I checked in. It's a nice room. I book a table at the Bella Sicily restaurant over the road and walk to the abbey ruins. It's chilly in the evening breeze, but the setting sun pours through the west window of the ruined chapel, gilding the old sandstone walls.

Monteviot suspension bridge

Market Place, Jedburgh

Jedburgh Abbey

Nave of Jedburgh Abbey

Day 3 Jedburgh to Morebattle

Tuesday, 13 May

I leave town, going north on a path along the River Jed. It's longer following the river meanders, but it gets away from the traffic. A climb up a country lane ends at a house and a diversion to the margin of a field of spring barley. The air is filled with birdsong – yellow hammer and white throat, as well as the usual suspects of robin, blackbird etc. The path joins Dere Street, now a grassy track through bits of woodland that drops down to a stream crossed by a wooden footbridge. There are benches, and a man with bare feet is reclining on one reading a book. I stopped to change into shorts, and he asked me where I was going. He's going all the way to Cape Wrath. He camped last night at Cessford Castle and was drying his tent on one of the benches. He's called Alec. I wondered if he'd done any other big walks in Britain and he mentioned the Coast to Coast. He's from Australia, in his 60s, I think, and going well.

Canongate Bridge, River Jed

Woodland Littledeanlees

Oxnam Water

There are small trout in the stream below the wooden footbridge over Oxham Water. I caught up with the Canadians on a grassy knoll after a climb out of the valley. Then, with the second lot of Canadians on a tedious, tarmacked hill. Don't look up, said one of the elderly women; it's too discouraging. I know what she means. At the top, the way mercifully goes left through a wicket gate into delightful woodland. It's shady and soft underfoot. There is a herd of brown cows with calves at the top and I stop to chat to the blind woman and her guide. There are marvellous views over Teviot Dale.

My lunch stop is on a pair of logs in a plantation of pine. I reach the road and get a view of Cessford Castle. I left my sack at the bottom of the hill and climbed to the castle keep. A compact plain cube of thick stone walls, still three or four stories high. Built about 1450, it was the principal stronghold of the Kerr family, notorious Border Reivers, many of whom served as Wardens of the Middle March. There was a long road into Morebattle, where I found a delightful, well-stocked community shop. I bought supplies and found the Old Dairy, where I was to spend the night. It had been renovated and was very swish.

Fox covert, Otterburn

Cessford Castle

Cessford Castle

Day 4 Morebattle to Kirk Yetholm

Wednesday, 14 May

A chilly start to the day, along a quiet country lane and across a wooden footbridge past a limestone cliff where they were mining sandstone and filling a trailer with road stone. The path ascends an unrelenting grassy path for 1000 feet. There were two figures ahead in the distance; I assumed they were the two women from New Jersey. I keep plodding upwards. It was steep, and I was out of breath. I glimpsed a hare crossing a field of newly sprouting cereal. Eventually, I reached the ridge, Grubbit Law and a final pull to the summit of Wideopen Hill (368m). The distinctive Iron Age hill fort and settlement of Hownham Rings can be seen to the south with the long ridge that the pennine Way follows in the distance. The two Americans are sitting on the grass against a stone wall. They are Presbyterian and on a pilgrimage. They say the Bishop of Toronto leads the

Grubbit Law towards Wideopen Hill

Canadian party. That must be Peter, who kindly gave me a lift in the coach.

A long, easy descent, steep in one or two places, then a mile or so along the road into Kirk Yetholm, then a pleasant path past a reed-circled lake. The Mill House, where I'm spending the night, doesn't open till four. It's 1.30, and David, the host, invites me to eat my sandwich lunch on the patio and to leave my pack while I wander into town. Whilst admiring the new windows in a stone barn, a lady invites me in and shows me the work her husband, a carpenter, has done renovating the three barns. It looks like a vast undertaking.

Tea at the Border Inn is more welcoming and nicer than I expected. The sun is shining, the village green looks inviting and all seems well.

Hownham Rings hill fort Windy Law with Lamb Hill and Pennine Way on skyline

Border Inn, Kirk Yetholm

The Kirk of Yetholm 1837

Day 5 Kirk Yetholm to Wooler

Thursday, 15 May

Breakfast at the Mill House was quite an affair, with nine of us sitting around a huge table covered in a thick linen cloth. Apparently, this was a cotton mill with 16 looms and one of the leading industries in the village. I bought a packed lunch, as it was impossible to make lunch from the breakfast offering. Claire, our host, is a good businesswoman, exhorting me to book directly, rather than through booking.com. They charge 30%, she said, and that is why people are giving up. The packed lunch, a tuna sandwich, crisps, an apple and homemade Flapjack, was somewhat pricey, but I was glad of it later, since the flapjack with its butter, syrup and sugar was like rocket fuel to tired bones.

A sign on the Green in front of the Border Inn said a tribe of gypsies had lived here in the 17th century. Today was chillier than forecast, and I had to stop in the bus shelter in Kirk Yetholm to put on my duvet. There

Start of the Pennine Way

was a short stretch of road before the long, grassy climb to the ridge. The song of larks ascending on rising thermals. The path here is shared with the Pennine Way for a mile before a parting of the ways. The great ridge of the Cheviots, that I had climbed to from Hethpool when starting the Pennine Way, ran away to the south across open moorland. Finally, I reached a wall and fence and a sign saying I was leaving Scotland and entering England.

I passed the farm, where Scharlie and I had stopped for our lunch five years ago, before starting the Pennine Way, because police were arresting people breaking the COVID curfew in Scotland. We had been seen by the farmer's wife, who said she would call the police on us. From Hethpool I looked up the valley I'd walked along, and it looked a long way, and I marvelled at my endurance.

The path winds over the grassy hills covered in gorse so thick that the smell of coconut is almost overpowering, and ancient blackthorn in blossom. A cuckoo in the distant wood, then a gravel track descending past a farm. I noticed walkers on the hillside to my right, and stopped to check the map, and realised I'd gone wrong and had to retrace my steps

Border England - Scotland

Arts and Crafts houses at Hethpool

Gnarled hawthorn and coconut smelling gorse

uphill, cut across a field and climb over a gate to regain the path. It's still chilly and there is a biting north wind. I'd like to stop, but there's no shelter, so I press on. Having been in the lead, I've now been passed by all the other parties. The two women from New Jersey are having lunch, and I stop briefly to chat and a little further on, I find a bum bag with a phone and wallet. It turns out to belong to one of the women. I stop for lunch at a hollow out of the biting wind and have a rest. The reviving flapjack does me the world of good, and I'm able to press on across the heather moorland. The paths would typically be very wet, but now they're quite dry. It's another four or five miles through woodland, and the path descends through recently felled pine woods, the huge stumps left to rot like a field of skeletons.

There's only a final short stretch of road into Wooler and Noble Lands, where I'll spend the night.

Brown's Law, approaching Wooler

Church Street, Wooler

Bed in Noble Lands apartment

Day 6 Wooler to Beal

Friday, 16 May, from Wooler to Beal

I bought a coffee and a pastry at the Perfect Shop cafe in the marketplace and stopped on the bench in the sunshine to have breakfast. The bench is next to a fountain. It seems that the original fountain, erected by public subscription by Robert Winteman 1870 to help combat a cholera outbreak, has been remodelled into a silly pastiche of a fountain and moved from the centre to the side of the marketplace. I imagine the discussion that there must have been in the local council about moving the old fountain, which may have been in the way of traffic. I returned to the cafe to buy a monster bun and a granola bar for lunch.

The way goes past the church and crosses the river before a Roman road leads to the hill and a delightful ascent, traversing the hillside on a narrow path through wildflowers. I reach a moorland of heather, blue sky

Water fountain 1870

St Cuthbert's cross

East Horton and bench made from tree felled in storm Arwen

WW2 pillbox at Mealkail Knowe

Large herds of cattle and lush pasture

Greensheen Hill

St Cuthbert's Cave

and skylarks. The descent is followed by an elegant bridge across the river and a long and tiring hill, through rich, productive farmland, arable and pasture with large herds of cattle and sheep, and big fields ripening wheat. The road is bordered by dozens of young trees planted in wooden paling tree guards. I stop at a bench made from trees felled in the recent Storm Arwen.

An endless, boring road climbing to a ridge on the skyline, then St Cuthbert's Cave, and a lunch break. It's warm in the sunshine out of the biting wind. The cave is a large overhang supported by a sandstone pillar. A stretch of moorland, then a grassy path past a small lake with two holiday huts, through pine woods and finally fields and the East Coast Main Line. A sign said you had to ring the signalman to get permission to cross. Slightly unnerving crossing the two fast tracks.

I discovered that the Lindisfarne Inn is not in Beal after all, even though the postcode was Beal, and I have to walk another mile or so to West Mains on the A1. It's a lovely day, so I don't mind even though my toes hurt.

St Cuthbert's Cave

Blawearie ruined farm complex

East Coast Mainline

Day 7 Lindisfarne to Berwick

Saturday, 17 May,

This is the last day of the walk to the Priory on Holy Island. There is a bus back to the causeway from outside the hostel. Soon after breakfast, I said goodbye to the American women, Lesley and Shelley. I told them about the bus, but they said that they were walking as a penance. A briefer time in purgatory, I suggest. Mine won't be brief, says Lesley. The bus is on time and stops obligingly at the causeway. It's still too wet to go across the sands, so I walk the sandy path parallel to the road. It takes a while, it's about four miles, but it is pleasant on the flat, with the pink flowers of thrift and sea purslane. I walk to the ruined priory and run into the Canadians. We're delighted to see each other. Peter asks what I thought of the hills. Wonderful, I say. he agrees. I get a coffee from a van on the way to the castle. It's instant and not that good, but it's chilly in the north wind, and I am glad of the warm milk. I walk to the castle, but don't go in, as

Overhanging cliffs

Statue of St Aidan, Lindisfarne, Kathleen Parbury, 1958

Lindisfarne Castle built c1550, remodllled by Sir Edwin Lutyens 1901

Lindisfarne Abbey ruin

Willow curlew sculpture, Holy Island

Refuge Holy Island Sands

View of Royal Border rail Bridge from bus entering Berwick

Berwick-on-Tweed Town Hall, Marygate

Quayside and Town Walls

Royal Tweed Road Bridge

I get a panini and tea in the cafe on the way back. I have time to walk back over the sands. It's delightful walking straight across the bay. I ponder a night in one of the box-like refuges on stilts halfway across. It would be interesting. A clear night sky would be something to behold. From the Causeway, The bus takes me to Golden Square in Berwick. From here it is a short walk to the King's Arms.

It's Saturday night and all the restaurants were booked, but a nice waiter at Mavi, a Turkish restaurant, squeezed me in. It was a warm evening and I wandered around the lanes and alleys of the old town, From the restaurant in Bridge Street down to the Old Bridge and the Quay. Its seems that Lowry visited Berwick regularly from the 1930s until shortly before his death in 1976 and captured the town in numerous paintings and drawings.

L S Lowry's favourite place

Day 8 Berwick-on-Tweed

Sunday 18 May

There was a problem with my room, I forget what, maybe the heating didn't work or there was a problem with the plumbing in the bathroom. Anyway they moved me to a much grander room on the ground floor at the front of the hotel. I was concerned it would be noisy, being on Hide Hill, a main street. But I slept well, once I managed to stop watching the Eurovision song contest and got to bed.

A late start and a walk to a cafe for coffee and croissant before wandering up Marygate to the station. The pavements with that lazy left-over Sunday morning feel with some people newly out of bed and a few souls thinking it might be time to get there.

Marygate early Sunday morning

Scotsgate, and Town Walls, constructed by Elizabeth I

Jubillee Fountain, Castlegate, J Whitehead 1880-85

St Cuthbert (c.634-687)

St Cuthbert (c. 634 – 687 CE) is the patron saint of Northumbria and one of England's most beloved saints. In his late 20s, he returned to Melrose and, on the death of his friend Boisil, he became prior at Melrose. Cuthbert moved to Lindisfarne at about the age of 30 and lived there for the next 10 years. He became prior of Lindisfarne Abbey in the 660s and was known for diplomacy and gentleness in guiding monks toward unity in reconciling Roman and Celtic Christianity after the Synod of Whitby.

Moved by the desire for a more contemplative life, around 676, he retired and moved to a place now known as St Cuthbert's Cave. Shortly afterwards, he withdrew to the island of Inner Farne to live as a hermit. One story tells how Cuthbert would spend long nights standing in the cold North Sea, praying. When he returned to shore, two otters would follow him, warm his feet with their breath, and dry them with their fur before returning to the water.

The Journey, sculpture by Fenwick Lawson, Millennium Square, Durham

In 684 CE, at the age of about 50, despite his reluctance, he was persuaded to leave his hermitage and become Bishop of Lindisfarne. He spent much time among the people, ministering to their spiritual needs, carrying out missionary journeys, and travelling from the North Sea to the Solway and from the Forth down into Lindsey in modern Lincolnshire. Cuthbert was famous for walking long distances, particularly to reach remote rural settlements. The Venerable Bede emphasises his preference for humble, personal contact rather than travelling with large retinues and stresses his willingness to travel in harsh winter conditions.

After a painful illness, he died on 20 March 687 on Inner Farne and was buried at Lindisfarne. Eleven years later, in 698, as part of a process of elevating him to sainthood, his sarcophagus was opened, and his body was reportedly incorrupt. In 793, Lindisfarne suffered the first Viking raid in England, when monks were killed, captured, and gold and treasure stolen. Lindisfarne was finally abandoned in 875, and the monks fled, carrying St Cuthbert's body with them around various places. After seven years' wandering, Cuthbert found a resting place at the church in Chester-Le-Street until 995, when another Danish invasion led to his removal to Ripon and finally to Durham, where the monks believed Cuthbert had directed them to found a new abbey. Cuthbert's shrine was destroyed by Henry VIII's commissioners in 1537, but they found his body incorrupt and hesitated to destroy his remains.

Henry's Commissioners, brought with them a goldsmith who, when he had taken off the gold, silver and precious stones, came to a chest strongly bound in iron. The commissioners commanded him to smash it open. "Alas, I have broken one of his legs". Dr Henley called out to him to throw down the bones but he could not because they were kept together by skin and tissue. Dr Ley went up and found the body was indeed whole and undecayed.

St Cuthbert's walk commemorates two key places in his life: Melrose Abbey (in the Eildon Hills), where he began his monastic life, and Lindisfarne (Holy Island), where he served as prior and bishop, and where he ended his days.

Cuthbert of Farne, Fenwick Lawson (b1932) English Heritage archive

Lindisfarne Gospels, produced 715-720, 30 years after St Cuthbert died

ITINERARY

No.	Day	Date	Start	Finish	Km	Miles	Ascent m	Accommodation
1	Sun	11-May	Hathersage	Melrose		221		
1	Sun	11-May	Melrose	St Boswells	6	4	20	Dryburgh Arms
2	Mon	12-May	St Boswells	Harestanes / Je	18	11	300	Royal Hotel
3	Tue	13-May	Jedburgh	Morebattle	16	11	357	Old Dairy Cottage
4	Wed	14-May	Morebattle	Kirk Yetholm	11	7	304	Mill House
5	Thu	15-May	Kirk Yetholm	Wooler	21	13.5	677	Noble Lands
6	Fri	16-May	Wooler	Beal	19.3	12	389	Lindisfarne Inn
7	Sat	17-May	Beal	Berwick	9.3	6	46	Kings Arms Hotel
8	Sun	18-May	Berwick on Tweed	Hathersage				
	Total				100.6	64.5	2093	

KIT LIST

Item	Make	Model	Notes	No.	Weight gm	Stars
Rucksack	Lightwave	Fastpac 30	Excellent, durable but very light.	1	992	***
Rucksac cover	Lowe			1	63	**
Note book	Moleskin		I always use these for my journals	1	111	***
Pens	Biro		Excellent	2	22	***
Phone	iPhone	12	Good battery life, excellent camera	1	75	***
Compass	Silva	with whistle	Excellent, very practical, have always used Silva	1	42	***
Reading glasses				1	22	***
Pocket knife	Gerber	Paraframe		1	54	***
Debit card			Essential	1	1	
Dry bags	Sea to Summit	Assorted	Excellent, durable and completely waterproof	5	310	***
Walking poles	Black Diamond	Distance flz	Excellent, light and well balanced	2	384	***
Sandals	Crocks		Useful for tired feet and getting into water	1	296	**
Water bottle	HydraPak 1L			1	100	**
Flask	Zojirushi				228	***
Pee bottle	Nalgene 1L			1	112	***
Sun cream	SunSense	Factor 50		1	30	
Toothbrush	CuraProX			1	25	
Towel	Mountain Warehouse	Ex Large	Plus mini Go face towel	2	151	**
Lenses, spectacles				1	90	
TOTAL KIT					**3,108**	
Boots	Sportiva		Wide fitting replacement boots bought in Corte	1	890	***
Anorak	Arcteryx	Alpha SV	Orange	1	506	***
Aerofoil softshell	Mountain Equipment				117	
Duvet	Frederick Anderson			1	292	***
Cap	North Face			1	86	**
Pants	Kühl		Excellent, fit well and good pockets	1	351	***
Shorts	Kühl		Excellent, fit well and good pockets	1	299	***
T shirts	Adidas		Excellent, stayed looking smart	3	450	***
Socks	Bridgedale		Excellent, very comfortable	3	0	
Underpants	M&S			3	46	
Swimming trunks	Speedo				90	***
Belt	Jukmo		Ratchet belt Essential, because you loose weight (6-7 kilos)	1	25	***
TOTAL CLOTHES					**3,152**	

TRAINING WALKS

Date	Name	Mileage	Km	Ht ft	Time hrs
06/07/2023	Black Hill	8.4	13.5	1758	5
23/09/2023	Cross Fell, North Pennines	9.1	14.6	2413	6
04/01/2024	Cheviot	6.3	10.1	2032	5
08/06/2024	High Cup Nick,	9.1	14.6	1648	6
28/06/2024	Spurn Head	7.5	12.1	96	4
24/07/2024	St Columba's Bay, Iona	8.8	14.2	1153	5
27/08/2024	Barmouth Bunkhouse	6.8	10.9	1810	4
28/08/2024	Cadar Idris	10.1	16.3	2978	7
04/09/2024	Stanage	4.1	6.6	710	5
22/09/2024	Mare e Monte, Corsica	57	91.7	1558	6
29/10/2024	Combe Dale	4.9	7.9	990	3
01/02/2025	Wardlow	6	9.7	519	3
25/01/2025	Nidderdale Moors	9.7	15.6	1594	6
31/03/2025	Chrome Hill	4.7	7.6	1205	3
09/03/2025	Lyme Park Moor	3.9	6.3	528	2
06/04/2025	Cold Fell, Geltsdale	11.7	18.8	1802	7
	Total	168	271	22794	77

www.ingramcontent.com/pod-product-compliance
Lightning Source LLC
Chambersburg PA
CBHW042338150426
43195CB00001B/39